ASHEVILLE-BUNCOMBE TECHNICAL INSTITUTE

From the Butchers Block

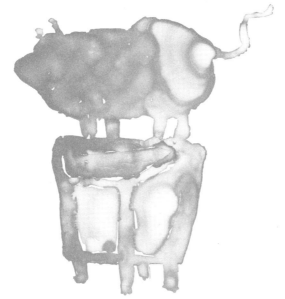

by Bonita Wagner

Westover Publishing Company   A Media General Publication   Richmond, Virginia

Meat is a very important part of our diets for both flavor and nutrition; and, thankfully, the average American consumes a fair amount of it. Fortunately, the various cuts of meat and methods of preparing them are, with a little imagination, almost un-ending.

But, because meat is also the most expensive part of our diets, selecting the proper cuts for the most favorable result is also important. Learn to select those within your budget and create new flavor combinations to spark different appetites.

So, don your favorite thinking cap with me and take on the challenge to choose the meats and types of cookery that cater to your family's palate and pocketbook.

Throughout this volume, I have included recipes for a wide variety of delectable entrees utilizing some elegant and some economical cuts of meat.

The word "sukiyaki," loosely translated from the Japanese, means "let's cook and eat together." There is joy in preparing this Oriental dish that is a meal in itself. Make it in an electric skillet at the table, adding the ingredients to the bubbling sauce to cook delicately for a very short time. You may want to use only half of the ingredients for the first service, then add the remainder as you eat so the meat and vegetables will not overcook.

Serve everyone a bowl of steaming hot rice and transfer the sukiyaki directly to the bowls from the skillet. And remember—chopsticks only!

Most of the ingredients required are available in supermarkets today, but those you may not be able to obtain easily have substitutions noted.

SUKIYAKI

Sauce:
1 cup beef consommé
$\frac{1}{2}$ cup shoyu (soy sauce)
$\frac{1}{2}$ cup mirin (cooking sherry or port wine)
1 heaping teaspoon sugar
$\frac{1}{2}$ teaspoon MSG

1 tablespoon cooking oil
1 Bermuda onion, sliced into $\frac{1}{4}$ inch thicknesses
12 scallions, cut into 2-inch lengths
2 cups shirataki (vermicelli)
4 large mushrooms, sliced
1 small can bamboo shoots, cut lengthwise into thin
   strips
1$\frac{1}{2}$ pounds beef tenderloin, very thinly sliced
1 bunch watercress (or fresh spinach)

Mix together all the sauce ingredients in a pitcher
and set aside. Heat the skillet to 250° F. and add
the cooking oil. Heat 1 minute, then pour in just
enough sauce to cover the bottom of the pan. Add
the Bermuda onion and scallions and cook 1 to 2
minutes. Add the remaining sauce, shirataki,
mushrooms, and bamboo shoots. Stir to mix with
other ingredients and cook until the vegetables are
half tender, 3 to 4 minutes. Add the meat and cook
until it looses its red color, 3 to 4 minutes. Add
the watercress and cook 1 minute.
Serves 4.

Though often considered rather pedestrian, meat loaf is a favorite of many and offers opportunity for great variety in preparation. This special recipe makes a moist and flavorful loaf because it includes fresh parsley, celery, and tomatoes.

For an encore, meat loaf makes superb sandwiches, hot or cold. To make hot open-face, wrap the loaf in aluminum foil and reheat in a warm oven. Heat a can of beef or mushroom gravy in a saucepan. Put a slice of the warmed loaf on white or rye toast and pour over about $\frac{1}{3}$ cup of the gravy. This makes a great Saturday lunch or quick "leftover" dinner.

It goes without saying that cold sandwiches made from meat loaf are good, too. Mayonnaise or a spicy mustard and some pickle relish or tomato slices will perk up a sandwich.

MEAT LOAF

2 pounds lean ground beef
$\frac{1}{2}$ cup each finely chopped celery and parsley
2 tablespoons grated onion
$1\frac{1}{2}$ teaspoons salt
$\frac{1}{4}$ teaspoon pepper
$\frac{1}{2}$ teaspoon oregano
2 teaspoons Worcestershire sauce
2 eggs, slightly beaten
$1\frac{1}{2}$ cups bread crumbs
1 1-pound can tomatoes

Preheat oven to 350° F.

In a large bowl, combine beef, celery, parsley, onion,
and seasonings. Then mix in eggs and bread
crumbs. Fold tomatoes into this mixture. Shape into
a loaf and place in a roasting pan. Bake $1\frac{1}{2}$ hours.
Allow to cool 5 minutes before slicing to serve.
Serves 6 to 8 generously.

A distinctive flavor of burgundy and herbs laced through this beef dish makes it one you'll surely want to serve when company comes. Little time and effort go into its preparation and accompaniments can be simple. Buttered noodles, a crisp salad and hot French bread, together with a glass of burgundy wine will make this an outstanding meal.

BURGUNDY BEEF

1 pound sirloin steak
$\frac{1}{4}$ pound fresh mushrooms, thinly sliced
$\frac{1}{2}$ cup dry red wine
$1\frac{1}{2}$ tablespoons butter or margarine
$\frac{1}{4}$ teaspoon each crumbled chervil, tarragon, and salt
$\frac{1}{8}$ teaspoon marjoram
$1\frac{1}{2}$ tablespoons flour

Trim the fat from the steak and slice the steak across the grain into $\frac{1}{8}$-inch-thick slices. Place the steak and mushroom slices in a small bowl and cover with the wine. Let this stand at least 15 minutes at room temperature, or 1 hour or more in the refrigerator. Drain meat and mushrooms thoroughly, saving liquid. In a frying pan, melt butter or margarine with chervil, tarragon, salt, and marjoram. Add meat; stir and cook over medium heat until the meat looses its pink color, 3 to 5 minutes. Add the mushrooms. Sprinkle with flour and blend in the wine marinade. Cook and stir until slightly thickened.
Serves 4.

For those who savor the flavor of peppy foods, steak au poivre (steak with pepper) is the ultimate. Cognac and a bit of Dijon mustard in the sauce enhance the appeal of this very special steak.

Serve with a mild vegetable such as buttered cauliflower or broccoli, a salad and crisp, hot French bread.

STEAK AU POIVRE

2 small 1-inch-thick boneless sirloin steaks (about $\frac{1}{2}$ pound each)
2 tablespoons whole peppercorns
Salt
3 tablespoons butter or margarine
$\frac{1}{4}$ cup cognac
$\frac{1}{4}$ cup light cream
1 teaspoon Dijon mustard

Trim excess fat from steaks. Crush the peppercorns in a plastic bag with the side of a knife or a rolling pin. Press the crushed peppercorns into both sides of the steaks. Sprinkle steaks with a bit of salt. Melt the butter in a skillet over a medium heat. Put the steaks in the pan and increase the heat to about 300° F. Brown about 5 minutes on each side for medium rare. Remove the steaks to a hot platter. Heat the cognac in the frying pan until just warm. Add cream and mustard and stir until all is mixed and well heated. Pour over steaks to serve.
Serves 2.

Roast beef and potatoes are good, but roast beef and Yorkshire pudding is superlative. Though it may seem that preparation would be difficult, Yorkshire pudding is actually quite fun and rather interesting to concoct.

One of the secrets lies in mixing up the batter while the roast is cooking. This allows the flour to "relax" for the duration of the roasting so the pudding will puff up nicely.

A good hot oven and plenty of crispy brown drippings in the bottom of the pan are also an important part of roast beef and Yorkshire pudding.

4- to 6-pound rolled rib roast

Pudding:
1 cup sifted flour
$\frac{1}{2}$ teaspoon salt
3 eggs
1 cup milk

Preheat oven to 325° F.

Place roast with fat side up on a rack in a roasting pan. Season if you wish. Insert meat thermometer into roast so that thermometer reaches thickest part of the lean meat and does not rest on fat. (A meat thermometer must never rest on fat or bone. Bone is too good a conductor of heat and fat is a poor conductor. It is the temperature of the lean meat that you want to gauge. Count on approximately 18 to 20 minutes per pound for a rare roast (140° F. on the meat thermometer), 22 to 25 minutes per pound for medium (160° F.), and 27 to 30 minutes per pound for well done (170° F.).

A 4-pound roast, rare, will take about $2\frac{1}{2}$ hours and a 6-pound roast, rare, will take about $3\frac{1}{4}$ hours. Cook roast to desired degree of doneness.

An hour before the roast is to be done, sift together flour and salt. In a medium-sized bowl, beat eggs with a rotary beater, then add the milk. Gradually beat in flour and salt mixture. Let this stand until the roast is done.

When roast is done, remove to a warm platter. Turn oven heat to 450° F. Pour off all but about 3 table-spoons of the fat left in the roasting pan. Return pan to the oven for 1 minute. Lightly beat the bat-ter for the pudding. Remove roasting pan from the oven and pour the batter in it. Bake pudding 20 minutes, or until it is puffy and golden brown. Serve immediately with the roast beef, a green salad, and a vegetable.
Serves 6 to 8 people.

A good old fashioned pot roast is great any time, especially in wintry weather, or when the budget is suffering a lean spell or when you want to sink your teeth into a hearty meal.

Pot roast is prepared by the braising method of cooking meats. This is the technique of first searing a piece of meat in some fat, then cooking it slowly in a liquid. Braising is particularly good for the less tender cuts of meat, such as those to be pot roasted, because the long, slow cooking in moisture helps to break down the tough connective tissues thus tenderizing the meat.

The basic ingredients for pot roast are beef, liquid, seasonings and vegetables. The variances for making pot roast are many, dependent on family tradition and likes and dislikes of certain flavors and texture.

The basic cuts of beef for pot roasting are many but look for chuck, arm, blade, or sirloin tip. These can all be pot roasted very satisfactorily.

The liquid required for cooking is usually water; however, red wine, beer, or tomato juice often are flavorful substitutes.

Seasonings range from salt and pepper through thyme, basil, bay leaves and so on. This area is particularly guided by individual tastes.

The vegetables to consider are generally onions and potatoes, either one or both. Not to be forgotten, though, might be carrots, turnips or even rutabagas. Still more adventurous in flavor is to try various fruits. Dried fruits such as apricots, prunes, raisins and plums are a delightful, refreshing change for a nonconventional pot roast.

First, the basic instructions for a pot roast which caters to the traditional palate. A few suggestions for substitutions are included. Serve this with buttered noodles or spaetzle.

OLD-FASHIONED BEEF POT ROAST

4 pounds beef chuck roast
2 tablespoons all-purpose flour
1 tablespoon cooking oil
2 teaspoons salt
$\frac{1}{4}$ teaspoon pepper
$\frac{1}{2}$ teaspoon dried marjoram, crushed
$\frac{1}{4}$ teaspoon each dried thyme, and dried basil, crushed or substitute 1 teaspoon prepared herb-blend mixture
$\frac{1}{2}$ onion, sliced
1 cup water (or $\frac{1}{2}$ cup water and $\frac{1}{2}$ cup wine or 1 cup beer)
3 medium onions, cut into sixths
1 pound carrots, pared and cut into chunks
1 pound (about 8) small potatoes, pared
$\frac{1}{2}$ cup water
$\frac{1}{2}$ teaspoon salt

Sprinkle flour over roast and rub it in. In Dutch oven, brown meat slowly on all sides in hot oil. Season with the 2 teaspoons salt, pepper, and the herbs. Add sliced onion and the cup of water. Cover and roast in 350° F. oven for 2 hours. Then, add vegetables and remaining water; sprinkle vegetables with the $\frac{1}{2}$ teaspoon salt. Cover and continue cooking 1 to $1\frac{1}{2}$ hours more, or until both meat and vegetables are tender. Remove to a platter for serving. Skim off the fat from the juices in the pan, and serve the juices, or make gravy.

To make gravy, add enough water to the skimmed juices in the pan to make about $1\frac{1}{2}$ cups. Combine $\frac{1}{2}$ cup cold water and 4 tablespoons flour in a shaker and shake well. Stir into juices, cooking and stirring constantly until the gravy bubbles. Season with a little salt and pepper to taste.
Serves 6 to 8.

For a different kind of pot roast that is surely a new twist to an old favorite, add dried fruits and some red wine to make a refreshing dish. This is particularly good served with hot steaming rice.

Leftovers (if there are any) from this pot roast have an especially good flavor because of the fruit. Makes great cold sandwiches with a little chutney or Dijon mustard.

FRUITED POT ROAST

3- to 4-pound beef arm or blade pot roast
2 tablespoons shortening
$\frac{1}{2}$ cup finely chopped onion
3 medium carrots, pared and cut into chunks
$\frac{1}{2}$ cup red wine
1 clove garlic, minced
$1\frac{1}{2}$ teaspoons salt
$\frac{1}{4}$ teaspoon pepper
$\frac{3}{4}$ cup each dried apricots and prunes
$\frac{1}{4}$ cup raisins
3 tablespoons all-purpose flour

In a Dutch oven, brown meat on both sides in hot shortening. Add onion, carrots, wine, garlic, salt, and pepper. Cover tightly and simmer 2 hours.

In the meantime, put the dried fruits in a bowl and cover with $1\frac{1}{2}$ cups hot water. (You can substitute a little wine here if you wish.) Let stand at least 1 hour. Drain, reserving the liquid, and place the fruit on top of the meat. Cover and cook another 45 minutes to an hour, or until meat is tender. Remove the meat and fruit to a warm platter for serving.

Skim the fat from the juices in the pan and serve the juices, or make gravy by pouring the skimmed juices into a measuring cup and adding the reserved fruit liquid to make $1\frac{1}{2}$ cups. Return the mixture to the Dutch oven. Blend together the flour and $\frac{1}{2}$ cup water and stir into the pan juices. Cook and stir until the mixture is bubbly and thickened. Serve with the roast.
Serves 6 to 8.

A one-dish casserole is often the answer when a crowd is coming for a casual dinner. In this tamale cheese pie, South-of-the-border-"casual" is carried out to the finest degree. To make things even easier for the hurried hostess, it can be made ahead to be cooked and served *mañana*.

A crisp green salad and cold beer complete this meal.

TAMALE CHEESE PIE

Filling:
1 tablespoon butter or margarine
$\frac{1}{2}$ cup chopped onion
1 clove garlic, finely minced
$\frac{1}{2}$ pound ground beef
1 cup sliced mushrooms or 1 8-ounce can, drained
1 1-pound can tomatoes
1 package frozen whole kernel corn, thawed
1 8-ounce can tomato sauce
1 tablespoon chili powder
Dash of red pepper sauce
$1\frac{1}{2}$ teaspoons salt
1 cup sliced pitted black olives
1 cup shredded sharp Cheddar cheese (about $\frac{1}{4}$ pound)

Crust:
$\frac{3}{4}$ cup corn meal
3 cups cold milk
1 tablespoon butter or margarine
1 teaspoon salt
2 eggs, beaten
1 cup shredded sharp Cheddar cheese ($\frac{1}{4}$ pound)

Preheat oven to 350° F.

Melt butter or margarine in a frying pan and sauté the onion and garlic. Add the beef and mushrooms; cook and stir until beef looses its red color. If a large amount of fat has accumulated in the pan, spoon some of it off and discard it. Add tomatoes, corn, tomato sauce, chili powder, red pepper sauce, and salt. Cover and simmer about 45 minutes. Add olives and simmer another 15 minutes.

Prepare crust by mixing together corn meal and 1 cup of the cold milk. In a saucepan, combine remaining 2 cups milk, butter or margarine, and salt; heat to boiling. Gradually add corn meal mixture, stirring constantly; cook until thickened. Cover and cook over very low heat about 15 minutes. Stir in eggs and 1 cup cheese; continue stirring until cheese is melted.

Line bottom of a buttered shallow 2-quart casserole with corn meal mixture, reserving 1½ cups for top of pie. Pour meat filling over corn meal mixture. Drop spoonfuls of remaining corn meal mixture over meat filling. Sprinkle remaining cup of shredded cheese over all. Bake 50 to 60 minutes, or until browned and bubbly around the edges.
Serves 6 to 8.

This pie can be prepared the day before and held in the refrigerator until time to cook, but be sure to allow another 15 to 20 minutes of cooking time if it is cooled.

The wonders of convenience foods are not to be slighted, for they often can save much time and effort at crucial moments. Certainly, the many interesting dry soup mixes available today not only serve in their specific role, but as bases for sauces and gravies as well.

Veal steaks cooked in a simple-to-prepare onion sauce make a hearty meal served with steamed rice, a green vegetable and salad.

VEAL STEAK IN ONION SAUCE

$\frac{1}{3}$ **cup flour**
1 teaspoon salt
$\frac{1}{4}$ **teaspoon pepper**
2 pounds veal round steak, $\frac{3}{4}$ inch thick
4 tablespoons butter or margarine
1 package dried onion soup mix
2 cups boiling water
2 tablespoons sherry cooking wine

Mix flour, salt, and pepper together and dredge veal steaks in the mixture. Save remaining flour for making gravy. Heat butter in a Dutch oven. Brown the steaks in the butter and spoon off excess fat.

Dissolve onion soup In water and add $\frac{1}{2}$ cup of this mixture to the steaks in the pan. Cover tightly and simmer 1 to $1\frac{1}{2}$ hours, or until steaks are tender.

To serve, remove steaks from pan and stir in remaining flour. Add sherry to the remaining soup mixture and stir into pan. Cook until thick.
Serves 4 to 6.

Lamb has a very distinctive flavor and is complimented by a number of other familiar flavors, the most popular of which is probably mint. However, many vegetables, such as tomatoes, eggplant, and zucchini are often served in combination with lamb.

The cuts of lamb are many and varied. Leg of lamb, the most familiar cut to most people, is a versatile piece of meat and can be enhanced with interesting flavors.

Less tender cuts of lamb and ground lamb also have a significant place on the menu.

Much of the influence on the ways we cook lamb comes from some of our foreign neighbors who use lamb considerably more than Americans.

Though often made with beef, authentic shish kebab should be made with lamb. A pungent marinade for the meat cubes and a combination of tomato, onion, mushroom, and green pepper interspersed on a skewer with the lamb makes a dramatic serving.

Shish kebab lends itself well to outdoor cooking and casual meal service. Arrange meat and vegetables, uncooked, in individual plates on the table, give everyone a skewer and let them make their own combination and grill it to their desired degree of doneness.

LAMB SHISH KEBAB

Marinade:
1/4 cup fresh lemon juice
1/3 cup water
1 teaspoon salt
1 tablespoon chopped fresh parsley
1/4 teaspoon grated pepper
1/2 teaspoon grated lemon rind
2 teaspoons Worcestershire sauce
1 small clove, garlic

Kebabs:
1 pound lamb, cut into 1-inch cubes
1 green pepper, cut into 8 wedges
8 cherry tomatoes or 2 medium-sized tomatoes,
    quartered
6 small white onions, parboiled
1/4 cup oil

Put the lamb in a bowl, combine all the marinade ingredients and pour over the lamb. Let this stand in the refrigerator at least 2 hours.

To make the kebabs, remove the meat from the marinade, pat dry, and put on skewers, alternating with the vegetables. Brush the kebabs with the oil and broil in preheated broiler or over hot coals 5 minutes; turn and broil another 4 to 6 minutes, or until meat has reached desired degree of doneness. **Makes 4 generous kebabs.**

The lively spices of a curry are so good. Combined with lamb and some special condiments, it is a combination that is truly tantilizing.

Serve curry with plenty of hot rice and little bowls of interesting condiments. Their extra flavors and textures are what really makes the curry. Chopped cashews, peanuts, shredded coconut, chutney, raisins, and watermelon pickle all make interesting and very appropriate accompaniments.

This is also a fine way to use the lamb left on a bone after a roast leg.

LAMB CURRY

2 to 4 tablespoons butter
$\frac{1}{2}$ clove garlic, crushed
1 small onion, chopped
$\frac{1}{2}$ cup chopped celery, including leaves
$\frac{1}{4}$ cup flour
1 to 2 teaspoons curry powder
2 cups milk
Salt and pepper
1$\frac{1}{2}$ cups cubed leftover roast lamb ($\frac{3}{4}$-inch cubes or
  pieces)

Heat the butter in a saucepan. Add garlic, onion, and celery and cook slowly until onion is lightly browned. Add flour and curry powder. Mix well and cook a few minutes. Add milk gradually, stirring constantly. Cook until thickened. Season with salt and pepper to taste. Add lamb. Serve hot.
Serves 4.

Note: If you don't have any leftover lamb, use about 2 pounds of boned lamb shoulder cut into 1-inch cubes. Sauté the meat in 4 tablespoons butter until it has lost its red color. Set aside and proceed as above. Add $\frac{1}{2}$ cup water when adding the milk, then simmer 1 hour, or until meat is tender.

A good meatball casserole is the perfect hearty winter time, after-the-game dish that will warm insides and have everyone coming back for more. This casserole has the touch of lamb for a different flavor idea and it's combined with a creamy mushroom sauce, made with old faithful, condensed mushroom soup.

LAMB MEATBALL CASSEROLE

1 pound ground lamb
2 eggs, slightly beaten
$\frac{1}{2}$ cup cracker crumbs
2 teaspoons bouquet garni (or equal parts dry mint,
  rosemary, and thyme)
1 teaspoon salt
$\frac{1}{4}$ teaspoon pepper
3 teaspoons salad oil
1 can condensed cream of mushroom soup
$\frac{1}{2}$ cup milk

Preheat oven to 350° F.

Combine lamb, eggs, cracker crumbs, 1 teaspoon of
the bouquet garni, salt, and pepper and mix well.
Shape into 12 balls. Brown in oil and drain. Arrange
the browned lamb balls in a 2-quart, shallow baking dish. Blend the remaining bouquet garni, condensed soup, and milk. Pour over lamb balls. Bake
$\frac{1}{2}$ hour.
Serves 4.

This casserole can be prepared ahead of time and baked when time to serve. Be sure to cook an additional 15 to 20 minutes if it has been cooled. This can be frozen also, and cooked from the frozen state.

Speedy elegance describes this lamb and mushroom combination that is perfect to serve company. Prepare the lamb chops with their stuffing ahead of time and keep them in the refrigerator. A half hour before serving time, remove from the refrigerator and let them stand at room temperature 15–20 minutes while the broiler is heating. These chops broil in only a few minutes, can be cooked on the grill outside in nice weather. Serve with a crisp salad sparked with some fresh mint leaves and some chewy pitta or Greek bread.

STUFFED LAMB CHOPS

1 cup chopped fresh mushrooms or 1 10-ounce can,
   drained
1 teaspoon instant minced onion
2 tablespoons butter or margarine
1 tablespoon dry sherry
$\frac{1}{2}$ envelope (2 tablespoons) sour cream sauce mix
4 1-inch-thick loin lamb chops
$\frac{1}{4}$ cup milk (optional)
1 tablespoon sherry (optional)

The butcher will cut the lamb chops to the thick-
ness you want. Ask him to slice a pocket in each
one, too.

In a small saucepan, cook mushrooms and onion in
the butter until tender. Stir in the sherry and sour
cream sauce mix. Remove from heat. Let cool 3 to
5 minutes, then fill each pocket with $\frac{1}{4}$ of the stuffing and close pockets with skewers or wooden picks.
Broil 4 inches from heat for 7 or 8 minutes. Turn
chops and broil 6 or 7 minutes longer.

To make additional sauce to spoon over the chops,
combine remaining sour cream sauce mix with $\frac{1}{4}$
cup milk and 1 tablespoon sherry. Heat together
and serve with the chops.
Serves 4.

When certain vegetables, like zucchini, are so abundant in the summertime, feature them as the entrées because they are at their very best.

For this zucchini, a flavorful lamb stuffing is a snap to mix up and the whole combination can be stored in the refrigerator until time to cook and serve.

This is a meal in itself. Serve with bread sticks and ice tea.

This is good served cold, too, as a lunchtime leftover especially during hot weather.

LAMB STUFFED ZUCCHINI

4 zucchini (6 to 8 inches long)
Boiling salted water
1 pound ground lamb
2 tablespoons fine dry bread crumbs
2 tablespoons catsup
$1/_2$ teaspoon Worcestershire sauce
$1/_2$ teaspoon garlic salt
$1/_8$ teaspoon pepper
1 egg, slightly beaten
3 tablespoons freshly grated Parmesan cheese

Preheat oven to 350° F.

Cut off ends of zucchini and discard. Scrub zucchini well. Drop into the boiling water and cook until just slightly tender, about 5 minutes. Remove from heat and plunge zucchini into cold water; drain. When cool enough to handle, cut in half lengthwise and scoop out pulp with a spoon, leaving shells at least $1/_4$ inch thick. Finely chop zucchini pulp and add lamb, bread crumbs, catsup, Worcestershire sauce, garlic salt, pepper, and the egg. Mix together lightly and heap meat mixture in zucchini shells. Arrange in a shallow baking dish. Sprinkle with Parmesan cheese. Bake, uncovered, about 30 minutes.
Serves 4.

A long time favorite of Count Dracula, this Transylvanian goulash made with pork and sauerkraut is a special treat. When the moon is full, serve it from your very best cauldron into big soup bowls with plenty of thick crusted rye bread and sweet butter on the side.

A chilled Hungarian white wine is the perfect accompaniment.

TRANSYLVANIAN GOULASH

3 tablespoons vegetable oil
2 pounds boneless pork, cut into 1-inch cubes
2 cloves garlic, cut in half
2 large onions, thinly sliced
2 1-pound cans sauerkraut, drained
2 teaspoons salt
$\frac{1}{2}$ teaspoon pepper
$\frac{1}{2}$ teaspoon dried thyme leaves
2 teaspoons caraway seeds
4 teaspoons paprika
1 cup water
1 cup commercial sour cream

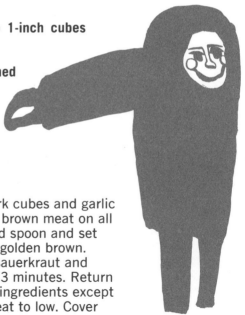

Heat oil in a large skillet. Add pork cubes and garlic and cook, stirring occasionally to brown meat on all sides. Remove meat with a slotted spoon and set aside. Add onions and cook until golden brown. Remove garlic and discard. Add sauerkraut and cook, stirring occasionally, about 3 minutes. Return pork to skillet. Add all remaining ingredients except sour cream. Stir together, turn heat to low. Cover

skillet and simmer 1 hour. Put a dollop of sour cream on top of each serving.
Serves 6.

Usually served with pork chops is applesauce. This dish substitutes the tart cranberry, and sweetens it with some honey. The blend yields a sweet and spicy combination that will inspire new appetites. Serve these chops with rice and buttered broccoli for pretty color contrast and fine flavor complements.

CRANBERRY PORK CHOPS

4 1-inch-thick pork chops
$1/_2$ teaspoon salt
2 cups cranberries
$1/_2$ cup honey
$1/_4$ teaspoon ground cloves
$1/_4$ teaspoon ground nutmeg

Brown the pork chops in a heavy skillet. Season with salt. Pick over and wash the cranberries. Grind in a blender or chop fine and put into a bowl. Combine with the honey and spices. Spoon this mixture over the pork chops. Cover the skillet and cook over low heat 1 hour, or until the chops are thoroughly done and tender.
Serves 4.

Great for parties, fun to concoct, and eat, lasagna is a hearty dish that everyone is familiar with, and few will pass up.

This recipe puts you to work making your own sauce from scratch, but the bottled jars of plain spaghetti sauce are an easy and legitimate alternative for the basic tomato and herb combination that makes up the sauce. This makes about 2 cups of sauce.

BAKED LASAGNA

$1\frac{1}{2}$ pounds Italian sausage or hot pork sausage, sliced
$\frac{1}{2}$ pound ground beef
1 cup canned tomatoes
1 15-ounce can tomato sauce
1 clove garlic, crushed
1 tablespoon basil
$\frac{1}{4}$ teaspoon cinnamon
2 teaspoons salt
$\frac{1}{2}$ teaspoon pepper
1 medium onion, finely chopped
1 cup chopped parsley sprigs
1 8-ounce package lasagna noodles
1 pound mozzarella cheese, thinly sliced
$\frac{3}{4}$ pound ricotta cheese
$\frac{1}{2}$ cup grated Parmesan cheese

Preheat oven to 350° F.

Brown sausage and ground beef in a skillet, breaking beef into pieces as it cooks. Combine tomatoes, tomato sauce, garlic, basil, cinnamon, salt and pepper in a blender until smooth (about half a minute on medium speed). Add onion and half of the parsley and blend until smooth. Drain the fat from the meat and add tomato sauce to meat; cover and simmer about 30 minutes. In the meantime, cook noodles according to package directions and drain well.

In a greased 2-quart oblong baking dish put a layer of about one third the noodles. Top with slices of mozzarella then dots of ricotta cheese and sprinkle on some of the remaining parsley. Pour over about $1/3$ of the sauce. Repeat this procedure, ending with a layer of noodles, then meat sauce. Sprinkle with the grated Parmesan cheese. Bake about 30 minutes, or until bubbly hot. Cut into squares to serve. **Serves 8 to 10.**

The tang and bite of a little hot mustard, some lemon juice and red hot sauce make this steak stand out in both flavor and fragrance. Simmer it long, over a low heat, and the flavors will blend and thoroughly penetrate the meat.

Serve with hot rice and a gelatin fruit salad to best compliment the unusual flavor.

PIQUANT STEAK

2 pounds chuck or round steak
1 lemon, cut in half
3 tablespoons butter or margarine
2 medium-sized onions, sliced
2 tablespoons Dijon mustard
3 teaspoons brown sugar
3 teaspoons Worcestershire sauce
3 dashes of hot pepper sauce
$\frac{1}{2}$ cup water or red wine
Salt and pepper
2 tablespoons capers

Cut steak into serving pieces, then rub with the cut
lemon. Melt the butter in a skillet and brown the
meat and onions. Combine the juice of the lemon,
1 teaspoon of grated lemon rind, mustard, brown
sugar, Worcestershire, pepper sauce, and water or
wine. Salt and pepper lightly to taste. Pour over the
meat and onions. Cover and simmer over low heat
$1\frac{1}{2}$ to 2 hours, or until meat is tender. Add the
capers during the last half hour of cooking.

To serve, remove meat to platter and pour juices
off into a small bowl to pass with the meat.
Serves 4.

"The meatballs make the spaghetti," an old Italian philosopher once said here's a recipe to make "a nice 'a spicy meatballs" and a basic tomato sauce with a secret flavor blending.

Cook up a package of your favorite pasta to serve with this. Make a crisp green salad with oil and vinegar dressing and crunchy garlic bread, too.

MEATBALLS AND SPAGHETTI SAUCE

Meatballs:
1 pound ground beef
$\frac{1}{2}$ cup bread crumbs
$\frac{1}{2}$ cup warm water
1 teaspoon garlic salt
1 heaping teaspoon oregano
1 tablespoon grated Parmesan cheese
3 tablespoons oil

Place ground meat in a large bowl. Add the remaining ingredients except oil and combine thoroughly. Wet hands and shape meat into balls about 1 to $1\frac{1}{2}$ inches in diameter. Heat oil in a deep skillet and brown meatballs well. Drain off most of fat; remove meatballs and set aside to drain.

Sauce:
2 6-ounce cans tomato paste plus 4 cans water
1 28-ounce can tomato sauce
1 heaping teaspoon oregano
1 tablespoon cinnamon
1 teaspoon garlic powder
1 bay leaf

To prepare sauce, combine tomato paste, water, and
tomato sauce in skillet, stirring to combine with
brown bits collected on the bottom of the pan. Add
the oregano, cinnamon, garlic powder, and bay leaf.
Simmer over low heat for 15 minutes. Add the
meatballs and bring to a boil. Turn the heat down
and let simmer, uncovered, 1½ to 2 hours. Remove
bay leaf before serving.
Serves 6.

Hint: To make meatballs that are all the same size,
shape meat mixture into a rectangle, cut into
squares, and roll squares into balls.

Few foods are better than good barbecued spareribs to pick up and gnaw to the bone for every flavorful morsel. The secret of good spareribs lies in selecting the leanest possible ribs, cooking off as much of the fat as possible, then adding a sauce that will enhance the pork flavor.

An Oriental spiciness makes this sauce particularly good. Serve these with rice and pour some of the extra sauce over it.

Ribs can be done indoors under the broiler or outdoors on the grill.

SPARERIBS FAR EAST

3 pounds spareribs, separated into serving size
  pieces
$\frac{1}{4}$ cup cooking oil
$\frac{1}{4}$ cup soy sauce
2 tablespoons lemon juice
1 tablespoon coriander seed, crushed
1 tablespoon instant minced onion
1 tablespoon brown sugar
$\frac{1}{2}$ teaspoon ground cumin
$\frac{1}{2}$ teaspoon ground ginger
$\frac{1}{4}$ teaspoon pepper

Preheat oven to 450° F.

Place a rack in a shallow roasting pan. Put the ribs
on the rack and bake in the oven 30 minutes. Drain
off the fat. Reduce the heat to 375° F. and bake 30
minutes more.

In a small bowl, combine the oil, soy sauce, lemon
juice, and spices. Spoon or brush the sauce over
ribs on all sides. Continue baking 1 hour longer, or
until ribs are tender, basting occasionally with the
sauce.
Serves 4.

If the flavor orientale doesn't ring your gong, a traditional American barbecue sauce is equally enjoyable. Follow the basic directions as above, but substitute the following sauce:

$^3/_4$ **cup ketchup**
$^1/_4$ **cup honey**
$^1/_4$ **cup wine vinegar**
2 tablespoons salad oil
1 teaspoon Worcestershire sauce
$^1/_4$ **teaspoon red pepper sauce**
$^1/_4$ **teaspoon salt**
2 tablespoons finely chopped onion
2 tablespoons chopped celery (optional)

Combine all ingredients in a small saucepan and simmer together 3 to 5 minutes before brushing on meat as directed.

These sauces are excellent on chicken or beef short ribs, too.

One of the less tender, but no less appealing cuts of beef are short ribs. Low heat and plenty of simmering time yield exceptionally flavorful ribs that make nice individual service for a party. Bathe these ribs in a wine sauce and serve with piping hot boiled potatoes, green beans and a salad.

BAKED SHORT RIBS

2 tablespoons flour
$\frac{1}{2}$ teaspoon paprika
1 teaspoon salt
$\frac{1}{4}$ teaspoon pepper
2 pounds short ribs
2 to 3 tablespoons cooking oil
1 cup red dinner wine (Burgundy is good)
1 cup water
1 clove garlic, diced

Preheat oven to 325° F.

Combine flour with paprika, salt, and pepper and roll the ribs in this mixture. Heat the oil in a skillet and brown the ribs well. Place the ribs in a $1\frac{1}{2}$-quart casserole. Combine the wine, water, and garlic and pour over the ribs. Cover and bake 2 hrs. or until tender.
Serves 4.

For a light late evening supper, a pilaf with an interesting combination of ingredients hits the spot. Pilaf, easily a meal in itself, is a combination of rice flavored with meat and spices. This one is particularly good because it also includes a bit of tomato flavoring to perk up the lamb.

LAMB PILAF

2 pounds lean, boneless lamb, cut into 1-inch cubes
4 tablespoons butter or margarine
1 large onion, chopped
$1\frac{1}{2}$ cups converted rice
1 $10\frac{1}{4}$-ounce can condensed beef broth
1 $14\frac{1}{2}$-ounce can sliced baby tomatoes
$\frac{3}{4}$ cup water
$\frac{2}{3}$ cup seedless raisins
1 teaspoon salt
$\frac{1}{2}$ teaspoon cinnamon
$\frac{1}{8}$ teaspoon pepper
$\frac{1}{2}$ teaspoon dried mint leaves or 1 tablespoon
  chopped fresh mint

Brown the lamb in a large frying pan in 2 tablespoons of the butter. Remove meat from pan and
set aside. In the same pan cook onion and rice in
the remaining 2 tablespoons of the butter until the
onion is soft and lightly browned. Stir the lamb,
broth, tomatoes and their liquid, water, raisins, and
seasonings into the rice mixture. Bring to a boil,
reduce heat, cover, and cook over low heat until rice
is tender (35 to 40 minutes). Remove pan from heat
and let stand, covered, for about 5 minutes. Fluff
with a fork. Serve on a bed of fresh mint leaves or
lettuce.
Serves 6 to 8.

Devilish ham inside and spicy bread crumbs outside wrap these veal steaks up in a whirl of flavors that will please any palate.

Serve them with buttered carrots, hot rolls, a salad and a glass of cool white wine for very special and elegant dinners.

DEVILISH VEAL ROLLS

4 boneless veal cutlets (about 1 pound)
1 4½-ounce can deviled ham
1 tablespoon chopped onion
1 tablespoon chopped parsley
1 3-ounce package cream cheese
1 10-ounce can or jar asparagus spears
1 egg, beaten
½ cup flavored bread crumbs
2 tablespoons butter or margarine
¾ cup water
1 envelope dehydrated mushroom gravy mix
¼ cup sherry

Preheat the oven to 350° F.

With a meat mallet or the edge of a plate, pound cutlets very thin. Mix the deviled ham with onion and parsley and spread ¼ of the mixture on each cutlet. Slice cream cheese into 12 narrow strips and evenly space 3 on each cutlet. Lay 2 asparagus spears between the slices of cream cheese. Roll cutlets jelly-roll fashion and fasten with wooden toothpicks. Dip rolls in beaten egg then roll in bread crumbs.

Melt the butter in a skillet and add the veal rolls and brown on all sides. Arrange the browned rolls in a baking dish about 10 × 6 inches and remove the toothpicks. Arrange the extra asparagus spears in between the veal rolls. Pour the water, gravy mix, and sherry into the skillet. Cook and stir until the mixture bubbles, then pour over veal rolls. Bake, uncovered, 45 minutes, or until the meat is tender.

Serves 4.

Purple plums add extra flavor and life to this leg of lamb, and greatly enhances its wonderful flavor.

Serve this with small whole potatoes roasted right in the pan to gain the flavor of both the lamb and the plums.

LAMB WITH PLUM SAUCE

1 5- to 6-pound leg of lamb
1 2-pound can purple plums
$\frac{1}{4}$ cup lemon juice
2 tablespoons soy sauce
2 teaspoons Worcestershire sauce
1 teaspoon crushed basil
1 clove garlic, crushed
1 8- to 10-ounce can small whole potatoes

Preheat oven to 300° F.

Salt and pepper the lamb and place it fat side up on a rack in a roasting pan. Insert a meat thermometer into the thickest part of the meat, but do not let it rest on bone. Place in oven and roast for 1 hour.

In the meantime, prepare sauce: Drain the plums, reserving $\frac{1}{2}$ cup of the juice. Pit the plums and purée in a blender or put through a food sieve. Combine with all other ingredients except potatoes.

After 1 hour of roasting is up, add the potatoes, and spoon some of the plum sauce and drippings over them. Baste the lamb with the sauce. Roast another $1\frac{1}{2}$ to 2 hours and baste 4 more times during that cooking period. Lamb will be well done when meat thermometer registers 180° F.; it will be a bit pink when thermometer registers 170° F.

To serve, remove lamb to carving board or platter. Skim fat from roasting pan residue and add remaining sauce to pan. Simmer until all is combined. Serve with the carved lamb and potatoes. **Serves 6.**

Stuffed cabbage is an Old Country favorite that is good to serve anytime. In cold weather particularly, its pungent tomato and cabbage sauce sparked with vinegar and sugar arouses both sense of smell and taste.

This is a suitable meal for a buffet, since it can be served nicely from a heated dish, is a hearty meal in itself, and is easy to eat if the crowd is eating from laps or TV tables. A green salad or applesauce and dark rye bread to soak up the extra sauce tops off this cold weather meal.

STUFFED CABBAGE

1 large head fresh cabbage
1 pound ground beef
$\frac{1}{2}$ pound ground pork
$1\frac{1}{2}$ cups cooked rice
1 small onion, finely chopped
1 teaspoon salt
$\frac{1}{4}$ teaspoon pepper
2 tablespoons sugar
2 tablespoons vinegar
1 8-ounce can tomato sauce
1 cup water
1 1-pound can tomatoes

Remove the bruised unusable outer leaves from the cabbage and cut the core out of the bottom. Bring a large pan of water to just boiling and place the cabbage in it. Simmer just until the leaves start getting soft and pliable. Pull or cut them off from the bottom a couple at a time to wrap around the filling.

To make the filling, combine the meats, rice, onion, salt, and pepper in a large bowl. Place about $1/3$ cup of this mixture at the base of each cabbage leaf. Roll the leaf one turn, then fold the sides in over the center. Continue to roll. Fasten the roll with a toothpick (but don't forget to remind eaters that the picks are there!). Continue to roll leaves in this fashion until all the meat mixture has been used. Place the rolls in the bottom of a Dutch oven. Chop coarsely any remaining cabbage and spread over the top of the rolls. Combine sugar, vinegar, tomato sauce, tomatoes, and water and pour over the cabbage rolls. Cover and simmer over a low heat $1^1/_2$ to 2 hours. Taste sauce and correct seasoning. If the sauce boils down too much, add some tomato juice.

Serve in a big bowl with plenty of room for the sauce. Pass a bowl of sour cream to top the cabbage rolls if desired.
Serves 6 to 8.

What to do with leftover ham (like leftover anything) presents a problem. With a little imagination and ingenuity, the bone, (a perfect candidate for the soup pot,) can be stripped nearly clean of good meat to combine in a pilaf that is a delightful medley of textures, flavors and aromas.

Serve this as a main course with just a salad and bread sticks.

HAM PILAF

2 tablespoons oil
1 onion, finely chopped
1 cup long grain rice
$2\frac{1}{2}$ cups hot chicken broth or bouillon
$\frac{1}{2}$ cup pecan halves
3 tablespoons chopped parsley
$\frac{1}{4}$ cup diced chutney (Major Grey's)
$\frac{1}{4}$ cup butter
$\frac{1}{4}$ pound mushrooms, sliced
$\frac{1}{4}$ cup flour
2 tablespoons Dijon mustard
$1\frac{3}{4}$ cups milk
Salt and pepper
3 cups diced cooked ham
$\frac{1}{4}$ cup dry sherry

Heat the oil in a skillet and sauté the onion until tender. Add the rice and cook, stirring, until rice is translucent, about 5 minutes. Add the broth and bring to a boil. Cover and simmer on a low heat 20 minutes. Then stir in the pecans, parsley, and chutney.

While the rice cooks, melt the butter in a saucepan and sauté the mushrooms for 2 or 3 minutes. Gradually stir in the flour to make a paste, then add the mustard. Stir in the milk and blend well. Bring to a boil, stirring constantly, and cook 1 minute. Add salt and pepper to taste, then stir in ham and reheat, but do not boil. Mix in the sherry.

To serve, spoon a portion of the rice onto a plate, then top with a serving of the ham mixture.
Serves 4.

From start to finish, the preparation time of this ham casserole should be less than 30 minutes. It's hard to beat for a meal-in-a-dish that is colorful and tasty, and its fine ingredients offer a wealth of vitamins and minerals. Double this recipe and it will make a colorful and tasty buffet dish for a dinner party.

CREAMY HAM COMBINATION

2 tablespoons butter or margarine
½ pound boiled ham, cut into ½-inch strips
1 can condensed cream of celery soup
½ cup milk
¼ cup mayonnaise
1 11-ounce can small peas and onions, drained
1 11-ounce can diced carrots, drained
2 1-pound cans sliced potatoes, drained
1 teaspoon dried parsley flakes
2 teaspoons prepared mustard
½ teaspoon pepper

Melt butter in a large skillet. Add the ham strips and cook over a moderate heat until slightly browned. Stir in the remaining ingredients and blend well. Cook over a low heat until mixture is heated through, stirring occasionally. Serve over a bed of rice or some nice hot buttermilk biscuits with a gelatin fruit salad.
Serves 6.

Never underestimate the versatility of bologna! As a sandwich filling, it is well established; and as an hors d'oeuvre component, it has been recognized; but as an entrée, perhaps it has not yet claimed its due.

Consider this the solution to a weekend evening supper dilemma, or the need for an impromtu dish for a Saturday lunch, or even for brunch.

OLD RELIABLE

$1/_2$ **pound sliced bologna**
2 tablespoons butter or margarine
2 medium onions, sliced
6 eggs
$1/_2$ **cup milk**
Salt and pepper

Leave the bologna slices in a stack and cut into 1-inch squares. Melt the butter in a skillet and sauté the onions until tender. Separate the bologna, add to the onions, and fry until the edges brown. Spoon off some of the fat, but leave about as much as you'd need for cooking scrambled eggs. Keep the skillet heated.

Beat together the eggs and milk in a bowl, add salt and pepper to taste, and then pour over the bologna and onion mixture in the skillet. Cook over low heat, stirring occasionally as you would for scrambled eggs. When eggs have set, turn out onto a platter and garnish with fresh parsley or carrot curls. Serve with toasted English muffins or good dark rye bread. **Serves 4 to 6.**

Spicy pork sausage seems to be in greater and greater abundance in the stores, suggesting perhaps that there are more uses for it beyond the traditional breakfast staple.

A hearty casserole, combining sausage and summer (or yellow crookneck) squash can be put together in a wink. The spicy sausage goes well with the mild squash. Some Parmesan cheese adds extra nip. This creates a casserole you'll want to serve often, particularly when fresh squash is available. Frozen squash can be used, though, if fresh is not available.

SAUSAGE AND SQUASH CASSEROLE

3 to 4 medium crookneck squash, about 4 cups,
   sliced
2 pounds spicy pork sausage
$\frac{1}{2}$ cup Parmesan cheese, grated
$\frac{1}{2}$ cup bread crumbs
1 tablespoon chopped fresh parsley
2 eggs, beaten
$\frac{1}{2}$ cup milk
$\frac{1}{2}$ teaspoon oregano
$\frac{1}{2}$ teaspoon garlic salt

Preheat oven to 325° F.

Wash and cut the squash into circles about $\frac{1}{4}$ inch
thick. Steam until just tender; drain. While the
squash is steaming, cook the sausage in a skillet,
browning it well and breaking it into small pieces
as it cooks. Drain on paper towels.

In a large bowl, combine the sausage and squash,
reserving several circles of the squash to arrange on
top of the casserole. Add the Parmesan cheese,
bread crumbs and parsley and toss together.
Combine the eggs, milk, oregano, and garlic salt and
pour over the other mixture. Fold all ingredients
together and turn into a $1\frac{1}{2}$-quart casserole.
Arrange extra squash circles around top of
casserole and sprinkle with a little more Parmesan
cheese if desired. Bake 25 to 30 minutes and serve
hot with a crisp salad and bread sticks.
Serves 4.

Good for family or for a crowd at a buffet, beef stroganoff is hearty and flavorful. A quick short cut to this great dish is accomplished with the use of canned, condensed mushroom soup.

This recipe calls for round steak, cut in strips, but a pound of hamburger meat can substitute, giving different overall texture making the cooking time shorter.

STROGANOFF

2 tablespoons butter or margarine
1 pound round steak, cut into thin strips
1 medium onion, sliced
1 $10\frac{1}{2}$-ounce can condensed cream of mushroom soup
1 $4\frac{1}{2}$-ounce can mushrooms, drained
$\frac{1}{2}$ cup sour cream
$\frac{1}{2}$ teaspoon paprika
$\frac{1}{3}$ cup water

In a skillet, melt the butter and brown the meat and onion well. Stir in the soup, mushrooms, sour cream, paprika, and water. Cover and cook over a low heat 45 minutes, or until the meat is tender. (Cooking time will be less, about 30 minutes, if you use ground beef.) Stir occasionally. Serve with hot buttered noodles.
Serves 4.

Marvelous things can happen under the broiler!
Here the zing of Parmesan cheese combines with
rich butter to bring out the very best flavor of simple lamb chops.

For a perfect accompaniment to prepare right under
the broiler, too, slice 2 firm ripe tomatoes in half
and sprinkle them with a bit of Parmesan and some
chopped fresh parsley. Slip them onto the broiler
pan next to the chops to broil along with the lamb.

BROILED RIB CHOPS

4 rib lamb chops
$\frac{1}{4}$ cup grated Parmesan cheese
2 tablespoons butter or margarine, softened
$\frac{1}{2}$ teaspoon salt
$\frac{1}{8}$ teaspoon pepper

Broil chops 3 to 4 inches from source of heat for
10 to 15 minutes, or until lightly browned. Turn;
broil 5 minutes, or to desired degree of doneness.
Combine remaining ingredients; blend. Spread on
chops. Broil 2 to 3 minutes, or until cheese is lightly
browned.
Serves 4.

If you've not had lamb shanks, and you like lamb, please try the next two ideas. They are truly a delight and should be added to everyone's culinary repertoire.

Though lamb shanks are not considered to be the most tender of the lamb cuts, when simmered slowly in a fine sauce, they become so tender the meat will almost fall off the bone. The sauce adds a unique flavor dimension.

Plan on one shank per person and serve with plenty of rice and a crisp salad with just a hint of an oil and vinegar dressing and maybe a sprig or two of mint.

LAMB SHANKS MIDDLE EAST

4 lamb shanks, about 1 pound each
2 tablespoons garlic salt
1 teaspoon pepper
2 tablespoons cooking oil
1 $\frac{1}{2}$ cups tomato juice
$\frac{1}{2}$ cup dry red wine
1 bay leaf
4 carrots, scrubbed and cut into large chunks
4 large celery stalks, scrubbed and cut into large
   chunks

Trim excess fat from lamb shanks. Combine garlic salt and pepper and rub into surface of lamb. In a deep skillet heat the oil and brown the lamb shanks on all sides. Add the tomato juice, wine, and bay leaf and heat to boiling, stirring occasionally.

Turn down to simmer, cover, and let simmer 45 minutes. Add the carrots and celery and simmer another 45 minutes to 1 hour, or until meat is tender. **Serves 4.**

You may put the vegetables in at the beginning if you want them particularly soft and flavorful. However, cooking them the lesser time allows them to maintain some of their crunch.

Another way to compliment lamb is with a piquant mustardy sauce that will not soon be forgotten.

LAMB SHANKS PIQUANT

4 lamb shanks
1 lemon, cut in half
Salt and pepper
1 tablespoon dry mustard
1 medium-sized onion, chopped
1 clove garlic, finely chopped
1 cup white wine or vermouth

Rub the shanks with the cut lemon and sprinkle with salt and pepper to taste, then coat with the dry mustard. Put the shanks in a large casserole so they lie flat on the bottom, if possible. Add the chopped onion and garlic and the wine. Cover and simmer over low heat 2 hours, or until the meat is tender. During the last hour of cooking, it is a good idea to remove the cover and turn the shanks around to make sure they are immersed in the sauce. Add more wine if necessary or desired.
Serves 4.

This classic Italian dish is simple to make yet conveys an aura of elegance that will grace any table, for family or guests. The secret of preparing veal this way is to treat it delicately during cooking, making sure not to cook it too long, as it will loose its tenderness.

This goes well with a scoop of rice, a green vegetable and hot rolls. Top it off with a super dessert, like a lemon cheesecake, to make an elegant meal.

VEAL SCALLOPINI MARSALA

2 pounds veal top round steak, thinly sliced and cut into 2-inch strips
Flour
$\frac{1}{2}$ cup butter or margarine
1 4-ounce can sliced mushrooms, drained
Marsala wine or a dry sherry
Salt and pepper
Lemon wedges

Dredge the veal strips with flour; then brown the meat quickly in melted butter in a skillet. Cover with the mushrooms and add enough wine to just cover. Simmer, covered, 5 to 8 minutes, or until meat is tender. Salt and pepper to taste and serve with the lemon wedges.
Serves 4 to 6.

Again, the convenient can of soup rescues the cook from extra kitchen time. Here, a delicious Swiss steak comes alive with a vegetable sauce right out of the can. Allow it to simmer very slowly to completely tenderize the meat.

Serve it with boiled potatoes or buttered noodles and buttered carrots.

SWISS STEAK

$\frac{1}{4}$ **cup flour**
$\frac{1}{2}$ **teaspoon salt**
Generous grating of pepper
1$\frac{1}{2}$ pounds round steak (about $\frac{3}{4}$ inch thick)
2 tablespoons cooking oil
1 10$\frac{3}{4}$-ounce can condensed vegetable soup
$\frac{1}{2}$ can water
1 cup sliced onions

Combine flour and seasonings; pound into steak with meat hammer or edge of a plate. Heat the oil in a large skillet and brown the meat. Pour off fat and add the remaining ingredients. Cover and simmer over a low heat 1$\frac{1}{2}$ hours, or until meat is tender. Stir occasionally.
Serves 4.

GREEK BURGER

1 pound ground lamb
2 rounds Greek pitta or Syrian bread (the flat, round kind)
1 large onion, finely chopped
4 to 6 tablespoons chopped fresh parsley or watercress
1 firm ripe tomato, thinly sliced

Dressing:
1 cup plain yogurt
1 large cucumber, finely chopped
1 teaspoon vinegar
1 tablespoon oil
1 teaspoon garlic salt
$1/4$ teaspoon pepper

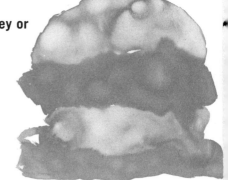

In a saucepan brown the lamb and cook until it has lost all its pink color. In the meantime, cut the bread rounds in half, then open at slit for filling. To make the sandwiches extra good, wrap the bread loosely in aluminum foil and heat for a few minutes in a warm oven. Combine all the dressing ingredients and let stand until you are ready to make the sandwiches.

When the meat is done and the bread heated, squeeze the sides of the bread half to open the slit for filling. Spoon in $1/4$ of the meat, top with some of the chopped onion, parsley, and a tomato slice or 2. Spoon on a couple of tablespoons of the sauce. Wrap in a napkin to serve.
Makes 4 sandwiches.